Raven's Gift

retold by Janice Kuharski
illustrated by Jo-Ann E. Kitchel

Richard C. Owen Publishers, Inc.
Katonah, New York

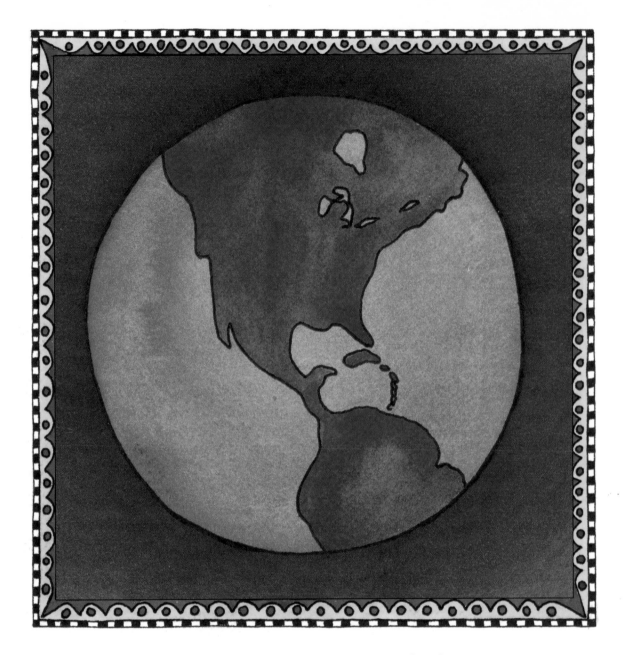

Long ago Earth was dark and dim.
There was no light.

The Chief of the Sky kept light
in a box in his lodge.

One day Raven said, "I must find a way to fool the Chief of the Sky and bring light to Earth."

Raven flew up into the sky
until he reached a tiny hole.

There he shook off his shiny black feathers, became a little boy, and laughed out loud.

The Chief of the Sky heard
the boy's laughter.

"How nice to hear a child's laughter," he said.
"The boy shall live with me in my lodge."

One day the boy began to cry.
He cried and cried and cried.

To stop his crying, the Chief of the Sky gave the boy the box that held light to play with.

"Thank you," laughed the boy through his tears.

Instantly, he became Raven again.

Down to Earth he flew,

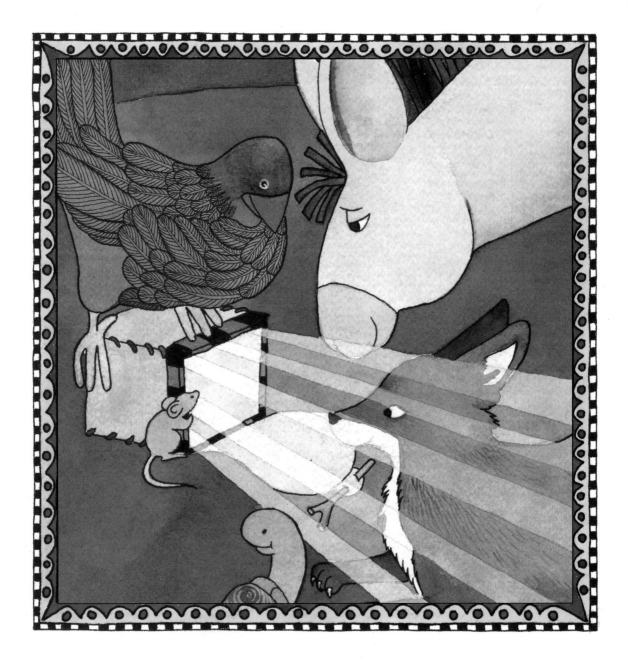

bringing light and color
to all the creatures there.